The Retirement Playbook
Strategies for Protecting Your Retirement Savings from High Taxes and Roller Coaster Markets

By
Marcus Warren

Introduction

For most of my life, I never imagined myself as a financial planner. My vision of a planner was that of my dad who was an accountant for CitiCorp back when I was young lad. Going into a quiet office building, working in a tiny cubicle, crunching numbers for clients 8 hours a day...BORING! No thank you. I'd rather work for my mom at the grocery store (which is what I ended up doing as soon as I turned 15).

But all that changed when I saw movies like _Wall Street_ with Gordon Gekko, _Trading Places_, _Glen Gary Glen Ross_, and _Boiler Room_. These are the movies that shaped my thoughts surrounding what it was like to be a financial planner or broker. Fast paced, phones ringing off the hook, and yelling out words like BUY, SELL, HOLD! It seemed sexy and exciting and I wanted to be a part of it.

So I applied to a national brokerage firm and found out very quickly that the Wall Street glamorized by Hollywood is much different from being a young broker in Louisville, Kentucky. No phones ringing, no yelling "buy, sell, and hold," and I'm in the south, so definitely not fast paced. As a matter of fact, when I first started, I didn't even have an office. I had to earn one by going door to door selling stocks and bonds and collecting the names, addresses, and phone numbers of potential clients. I quickly realized that I wasn't on Wall Street. Actually, I was 739 miles away.

So here I am now, almost 20 years in this business and wow, how the financial planning industry has changed. We've gone from a sales force based industry (like in *Boiler Room*) that hoarded information and sold stock trades, research, and investment management, to more holistic planning where we're advising clients not just on investments, but basing our value proposition on the entirety of a client's full financial life.

And that's why I wrote this book. Because the old paradigm of retirement planning has changed and as the new paradigm starts to set in, **retirees have to be prepared**. And that's my mission and purpose, to make sure that you are prepared for a retirement that is going to look much different from your parents' version.

Gone are the days of working for the same company your whole career, then retiring with a gold watch and a pension. The new paradigm suggests that you'll work for multiple companies during your career, you will not have a pension, and you will be responsible for your retirement through some sort of employee-directed retirement plan.

Retirees these days are living a lot longer than their parents did and will need their money to last a lot longer. Retirement is about INCOME. Income that will increase and keep up with inflation and income that will last as long as you do. And with this new paradigm shift and risk shift from the employer to the employee, you need to be ever more astute with how you save for this new reality in retirement.

Retirement Reality

If you're afraid you haven't saved enough for a secure retirement, you're not alone. The American ideal of a happy, secure retirement is under threat as the economic changes and the financial underpinnings that supported previous generations deteriorate.

Americans are increasingly anxious about obtaining the financial means and savings necessary for a solid retirement.

In the days of old, we generally had three potential sources of income after leaving the workforce: Social Security, private pensions and personal savings.

That trio—sometimes called the "three-legged stool" of retirement—is now in trouble. Social Security, which was never designed to be the sole source of income in retirement, provides only a fraction of a retiree's income, and we all have heard that it is at risk of running out of money in the decades ahead unless changes are made to its funding or benefits.

Traditional pensions that guarantee a fixed monthly sum for life have largely become extinct (like the dodo bird) for workers younger than baby boomers.

And personal savings, including employer-sponsored retirement plans, have funds well short of what most Americans will need to maintain their standard of living once they retire.

The result is that retirement is increasingly a "do-it-yourself" proposition and personal retirement savings are an ever more important part of the equation. That would be fine if we were saving more, but we are saving less.

A Retirement Crisis is on the Horizon

Ultimately, the shift from defined benefit pension plans to employee-directed plans, such as 401(k)s is the major driver of the impending retirement crisis. Beginning in the 1980s, this move helped companies reduce their retirement liabilities, **but it put an unmanageable burden on employees**. For 401(k)s to be effective, contributions must be made consistently throughout a worker's career. And we all know that being consistent is tough for us Americans. So people tend to make contributions sporadically and they also struggle with choosing contribution levels and investment options.

BONUSES

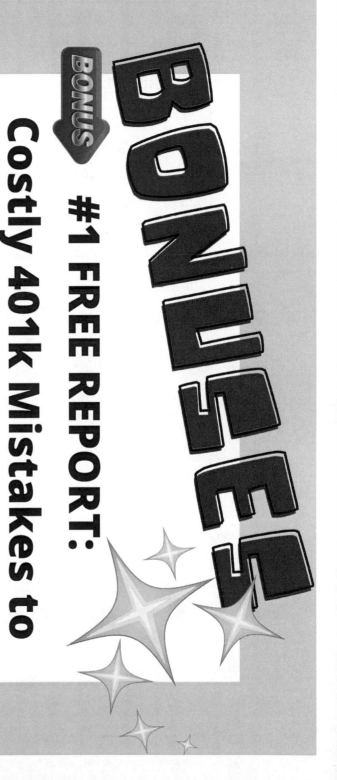

BONUS

#1 FREE REPORT:

Costly 401k Mistakes to

Avoid

visit bit.ly/rollovermistakes

BONUS

#2 FREE WORKSHOP:

TAXES IN RETIREMENT

Held on June 22 at 6:00pm

Indiana Wesleyan Louisville Campus

MUST RSVP: 502-286-6300

More info: www.financialea.org

Questions? Call us at 502-339-8255

Even when contributions are made, 401(k)s tend to earn lower than average returns due to limited investment strategies and high administrative fees. Employees in these plans often do not have significant investing expertise and earn rates of return that are substantially below professionally managed pension plans. And when workers near retirement and need to decide how to withdraw funds, determine a spending rate, and map out an investment strategy, **many lack the expertise to do so effectively**. The result is that many workers are left with insufficient nest eggs for retirement.

So, enough with **the doom and gloom**. This book is designed to shed light on retirement and all the things to take into consideration when planning for it. Retirement is about _peace of mind_ that you have saved enough money, _peace of mind_ that your money is going to keep up with inflation and more importantly, _peace of mind_ that your money is going to last as long as you do. We are living a lot longer these days, 70 is the new 60 and 60 is the new 50. Heck, Betty White is 137 years old and is in the prime of her life!

Seriously though, the paradigm of retirement has changed. In this technological age, we are all drowning in information from the *Wall Street Journal* to all of the financial networks and of course, the Google machine. But, what we are all lacking is knowledge and wisdom. Retirees need to be equipped with information to navigate these sometimes rough and murky waters. Hopefully, after you read this book, you will walk away with the insight needed to take action and have a prosperous retirement.

Lesson Number One: There is No Nostradamus

"Uncertainty is the only certainty there is, and knowing how to live with insecurity is the only security."

–John Allen Paulos

Imagine a TV network dedicated to fortune telling. Every day, it features highly educated people who strongly believe they can predict the future. Like Isaiah, they offer their prophecy for free. Unlike Isaiah, these seers are wrong about 80% of the time. Yet, despite the failures, viewers continue to watch. Even worse, many stake their entire personal fortunes on the advice.

Would you watch such a network? Millions do. In fact, there isn't just one such channel, but two: Fox Business Channel and CNBC.

Go ahead...turn them on, especially around noon on a weekday. These channels bring on one market "expert" after another to give out stock tips or some insight as to where the market is headed.

Here's a little reality: No one...and I mean no one...knows where investment markets are headed in the next week, month, or year. If they did know, they certainly wouldn't tell you for free. In fact, they wouldn't tell you at all because such information would be far too valuable to even sell.

Remember the rule of transitive properties from math class? If A is greater than B...and B is greater than C, then A is also greater than C. Or to put it another way, if Bill is taller than Mike, and Mike is taller than Jim, then Bill is also taller than Jim. Got it?

Okay...now pay very close attention.

Markets react to news. Do you agree? Every time stocks drop in price, isn't there always some news event attributed to it? Recall 9/11, Microsoft anti-trust suit, the Fed raising interest rates, earnings reports lower than expected?

News is unpredictable. Do you agree? Did you know any of the following events would happen before they actually occurred?

1. Hijacked airplanes crashing into the World Trade Center and the Pentagon.
2. The Kennedy Assassination.
3. The announcement of Toxic Asset Relief Program.
4. Arthur Anderson's false accounting of Enron.
5. Pearl Harbor (okay...this one isn't fair. You probably weren't alive).

In response to each of these news events, equity markets dropped rapidly. If you did know about these events a week before they actually occurred, you could have made billions of dollars.

Two movies come to mind that demonstrate this reality.

Casino Royale (2006): James Bond seeks to defeat a card playing terrorist who makes huge rates of return by shorting stocks on companies and then staging acts of sabotage on those corporations because he knows it will drive down their stock price. In other words, he knows the news before anyone else because he's creating it.

Wall Street (1987): Gordon Gekko hires aspiring trader Bud Fox to "stop sending me information and start bringing me some." So, Bud breaks into offices at night, spies on company executives, and relays insider information told to him by his father. As a result, Gekko has "news" that no one else has, allowing him to trade ahead of the market.

So, if news is unpredictable and market performance reacts to news, then market performance is unpredictable.

Wait a minute. Are you saying then that all those Wall Street experts like Jim Cramer and Charles Paine really have no idea what they're talking about?

Yes...and no. They certainly know many things. But so do millions of other traders. Everything they know is already factored into a stock's price. It's what they don't know, the future news, which will drive stock prices. They are simply speculating as to what they think the news will be.

Sometimes they get it right...most of the time they get it wrong. Studies show that on average 80% of all professional portfolio managers fail to beat their benchmark index. Of the 20% who do, very few repeaters exist.

The Law of Large Numbers

Imagine we fill the Cardinal Stadium with 35,000 people. On the PA system, we instruct them all to stand up and remove a quarter from their pocket.

On our mark, they all flip the coin. Those who flipped heads (about 17,500) remain standing. Those who flipped tails sit down. We now repeat this exercise, again and again. With 35,000 people flipping coins, we are willing to bet our houses that at least one person in the stadium will flip heads ten straight times. In fact, we wouldn't be surprised if at least 20 people did it.

The law of large numbers states that if you have enough people try to do something, then someone will succeed regardless of skill level. The individual who tossed heads 10 straight times...is he an expert coin flipper? Does he somehow understand the gravitational properties between his quarter, his wrist, and the earth? Or was he just lucky?

Guess how many professional portfolio managers exist today? Yup...about 35,000.

Over 2,000 work for Fidelity alone. Someone is bound to speculate correctly on the market's reaction to news that has yet to occur.

The successful coin flipper is called lucky. The successful stock picker is called a guru and gets his face on magazines.

Again, we'll concede that these people are smart. Most went to the very best business schools in the country where they were taught that markets and stock prices are not predictable. But when they arrived on Wall Street, they were told how their firms really make money: trades.

Over 1 billion trades a month at $9 per trade on the New York Stock Exchange alone. You do the math. It is in *their* best interest to trade...not yours.

We do think that these very smart people honestly believe they have found a peek into the future. If there were only a handful of them researching companies, then they might actually be onto something. But there exist thousands, all crunching the same data. Furthermore, their efforts to buy and sell ahead of the market incur costs that lower their rates of return.

In 2013, Eugene Fama won the Nobel Prize in economics for stating in the 1960's that something is worth only what someone is willing to pay for it. Called "The Efficient Market Hypothesis", Fama showed (with a bunch of math) that the current price of a stock or bond is the correct price. Nothing is overvalued or undervalued until someone offers or agrees to a different price.

If you buy a house for $300,000, spend $50,000 for improvement, and put it up for sale, how much is it worth if the highest offer you receive is $290,000?

Correct. It's worth $290,000.

So if it's true for real estate, why not stocks?

The $6 watch

Zach Norris is a young man with a passion for fine watches. Understanding that people often don't know the value of their old jewelry, he routinely visits thrift shops and garage sales looking for great deals. If he sees a watch that he knows he can quickly resell for a profit, he will buy it for the asking price and then quickly find a new buyer. In January of 2015, he bought a $6 watch at his local Goodwill store and then sold it for $35,000.

Norris is to watches what Wall Street portfolio managers aspire to be to stocks. But unlike Mr. Norris, they deal in public information. Had Goodwill known the watch was worth $35,000, would they have sold it for $6? Or, would the prior owner have given away the watch to Goodwill in the first place? Of course not. Mr. Norris had insider knowledge. In this case, he can legally act on it. But in the world of security trading, such a move can land you in jail (see Martha Stewart and Bud Fox).

Perhaps there was a time when news traveled slowly enough for someone to get a jump. Those days are over.

There is no Nostradamus. News occurs randomly, and so too will stock and bond prices. All we have going for us is that, over the history of mankind, good news has outperformed bad. Despite world wars, famines, epidemics, assassinations, national debt, and disco, capitalism finds a way to improve the quality of life. The quality of your life today dwarfs that of every king and queen of the middle ages. It dwarfs that of your great grandparents, and even your grandparents. Is it not only logical to assume that in the future, we will witness massive amounts of bad news, but we will prosper despite it?

We don't need Nostradamus to conclude that leaning on optimism is the realistic way to view the future. Hence, actions like market timing and stock picking are far less likely to succeed than buying, holding, and rebalancing a broadly diversified portfolio.

Don't Just Take My Word For It:

The Investment Answer by Daniel Goldie and Gordon Murray

Random Walk Down Wall Street by Burton Malkeil

The Smartest Investment Book You'll Ever Own by Dan Solin

What Wall Street Doesn't Want You to Know by Larry Swedroe

Winning the Loser's Game by Charles Ellis

Lesson Number Two: Yes, You Will Use This Someday

"Mathematics are well and good, but nature keeps dragging us around by the nose."

–Albert Einstein

You remember your high school math teacher – that matronly woman who has been teaching out of the same book for thirty years because "the math hasn't changed." As you looked at the inside cover of the book, you saw the names and years of the prior holders. "Was it as boring for Fred Saddlemire in 1968 as it is for me now?" you asked yourself.

The one question that rose above all others was, "Will I ever need to know this stuff?"

She assured us we would. Now you're about to see she was right.

Meet Hans & Franz. When not pumping iron and injecting themselves with steroids, they are drawing income from their savings accumulated from years on late night TV. Aside from an occasional State Farm commercial, the two are pretty much retired.

Convinced that no one should invest like a girlie man, Hans has invested heavily in equities under the belief that over time, he stands to earn a higher rate of return. Chances are he'll be right.

Franz is no stranger to machismo, but opts for a portfolio that is likely to produce a lower, but more consistent rate of return. Starting with one million dollars each, they both desire to withdraw $50,000 per year to supplement their SNL royalty checks.

Hans and Franz are about to learn what Mrs. Cheeseman taught us years ago.

Average return may not be as important as consistency of return.

Hans: $1,000,000			
Year	Withdrawal	Return	Y/E Value
1	$50,000.00	-13	$826,500.00
2	$50,000.00	-20%	$661,200.00
3	$50,000.00	5%	$694,260.00
4	$50,000.00	-7%	$599,161.80
5	$50,000.00	20%	$658,994.16
6	$50,000.00	25%	$761,242.70
7	$50,000.00	-25%	$533,432.03
8	$50,000.00	45%	$700,976.44
9	$50,000.00	30%	$846,269.37
10	$50,000.00	20%	***$908,060.56***
Return Average: 8%			

Franz: $1,000,000			
Year	Withdrawal	Return	Y/E Value
1	$50,000.00	6%	$1,007,000.00
2	$50,000.00	8%	$1,087,560.00
3	$50,000.00	7%	$1,163,689.20
4	$50,000.00	11%	$1,236,195.01
5	$50,000.00	-4%	$1,138,747.21
6	$50,000.00	6%	$1,154,072.04
7	$50,000.00	12%	$1,236,560.69
8	$50,000.00	-2%	$1,162,829.48
9	$50,000.00	10%	$1,224,112.42
10	$50,000.00	6%	***$1,244,559.17***
Return Average: 6%			

As you can see, although Hans indeed earned a higher average return (8% vs. 6%) at the end of ten years, he has considerably less money than his body-building brother. Why? Every year, the two sell a part of their portfolios' shares to generate cash. When shares rise in value, it requires fewer shares to generate $50,000. When share prices fall, we must sell more. Those extra shares, once sold, are gone. It matters not what a portfolio does in the future in relation to those shares. They will never return.

By minimizing his potential downside, Franz has more money even though he averaged less over time. Fewer negative years means he sells fewer shares.

This phenomenon exists only because Hans and Franz need to sell shares for cash. Had they never needed to take money, then Hans would have much more money than Franz, despite the volatility. This is the **Math of Retirement.**

High school statistics taught us that nothing in life performs consistently--not the weather, not your golf score, and certainly not an investment portfolio. This lack of consistency can be measured. It is called *standard deviation*. The lower the standard deviation, the more likely you will earn the average return each and every year. So, if you find a portfolio with a guaranteed return of 8% every year, then the standard deviation is zero. Good luck finding that. Chances are, the best you'll do in seeking your 8% is a portfolio with a standard deviation of ten. So, what does that mean?

<u>If Average Return is 8% and Standard Deviation is ten, then:</u>

66% of the time: You will have a one year return between -2% and 18%.

95% of the time: You will have a one year return between -12% and 28%.

99% of the time: You will have a one year return between -22% and 38%.

If you are an investor, then your portfolio also has a long-term average return and a standard deviation to go along with it. The problem is that very few people know this, nor do they understand the "normal" volatility that comes with it. If they did, I think they'd be much less likely to panic.

For example, if a portfolio has the dimensions described in the chart above, should we be surprised (or even disappointed) if we earn a return of -6% in a given year?

Of course not. We already know going in that this is very likely. We also know that over time, it's more likely that we'll have more positive results than negative results. Guaranteed? No. Likely? Yes.

Think of it like baking a cake. You can put in the best ingredients, but all you have is liquid unless you put the batter in the oven for the right amount of time.

Results do not come in a linear fashion, no matter how badly we wish they did. What in life does? Do the giant redwoods of northern California grow the same number of feet every year? Does it take you the same number of minutes to drive to work each day? Do farmers dig up their corn seeds every few days to see if they are sprouting, or have they learned to trust the process?

It is essential that you know the long term average return and standard deviation of your portfolio allocation. Without knowing, you are simply winging it; and your survival mechanism stands a much better chance of overriding your logic.

Know your math. Make your high school math teacher proud!

Don't Just Take My Word For It:

The Intelligent Asset Allocator by William Bernstein

All About Asset Allocation by Richard Feri

Asset Allocation by Roger Gibson

Lesson Number Three: The Boogeyman is Real

"The only two things that scare me are God and the IRS"

–Dr. Dre

Assuming that you do not define patriotism by the amount you pay in taxes, what follows should be useful.

If you're one of the 53% of Americans who pay federal income taxes, then it is likely you pay more than what is legally required. If you own a small business, then it's almost a certainty you are over paying.

The Seven Most Expensive Words in the English Language: My CPA takes care of my taxes.

From our experience, most CPAs do a great job of filing taxes; but very few actually do any real tax planning. I ask people when the last time their CPA said he found a way to lower their taxes by $4,000, and they usually give me a blank stare and say, "Never."

Does your CPA/Tax Preparer ever:

- Call you with proactive strategies to achieve a tax-free retirement?

- Demonstrate how to restructure your 401k/403b/IRA accounts to avoid future taxation?

- Advise how to collect your Social Security benefits TAX FREE?

- Show you how to structure your business to minimize employment taxes?

- Show you how to write off your family's medical bills as a business expense?

- Show you how you can hire children (or grandchildren) to shift income from yourself to them?

- Help you choose the right retirement plan for your business?

- Explain how each of your investments is taxed and make suggestions on how to reduce them?

- Advise you on how to carefully consider which investments belong in **taxable accounts** and which investments belong in **tax-advantaged accounts**?

- Develop a plan for maximizing the value of any long-term capital loss carryforwards?

- Explain the rules governing "passive" income and losses and have a plan to avoid "suspended" losses?

- Meet with you throughout the year to discuss your business--or does he just wait until taxes are due?

- Give you a plan for minimizing taxes-- or does he/she just wing it every year?

Aside from investing behavior, income taxes are the greatest obstacle to most investors. There is never an age at which you stop paying them. You paid tax on your Social Security as you put money into the system, and you will likely pay tax on the money as it comes out.

When you reach age 70.5, you must start paying tax on your retirement plans (401k, IRA, 403b). When you die, your heirs must also pay tax on whatever is left.

Your estate may be taxed again for simply being too big.

The code is, by design, very complicated. Too often, people just go along with it, unaware of the steps that can legally reduce their federal and state income taxes. This is especially important during retirement.

You have a choice of paying taxes now...or later. To many, procrastination seems logical when it comes paying the IRS. For years people have socked away massive amounts of money in 401ks, 403bs, IRAs. The idea is you invest it now in a tax deductible/tax deferred account while you're in a high tax bracket. Then you withdraw it at a lower tax bracket when you retire. *Or so you hope*.

But what if taxes rise in the future? Our country, as of 2018, owes over $21 trillion. Projections suggest this amount will continue to rise as more and more baby boomers retire. Fewer people will be paying taxes and more will be requiring things like Medicare, Medicaid, and Social Security. A historical look at tax rates shows that the top marginal rate has been upwards of 70%, 80%, even as high as 94%. Today it's 37% (at least until the recent tax cuts expire). We've had much higher taxes in the past. We should be prepared for them in the future.

So how can this affect your retirement savings? A quick Case Study will demonstrate the impact.

Case Study

Bill and Karen Tucker are both 65. Retired, Bill has a rollover IRA worth $600,000. Bill collects $2,200 a month from Social Security. Karen receives $1,800.

They need $7,000 each month to live comfortably, so they withdraw $3,000 per month from their retirement accounts.

To determine how much of their Social Security check is subject to taxation, we add the annual IRA withdrawals ($36,000) to one-half of the Social Security payments ($24,000).

This gives them a modified adjusted gross income (MAGI) of $60,000.

Whenever the MAGI for a married couple exceeds $44,000, then **up to 85%** of their Social Security check is subjected to taxation.

Assuming they file jointly and use the standard deduction, Bill and Karen owe about $4,000 in Federal income taxes.

Almost half of their Social Security benefits are included in their taxable income!

Now, what if they had decided a few years back to convert their rollover IRA to a Roth

IRA? Doing so would have triggered tax at the time of conversion, but no tax would ever be owed on the accounts again. Even if their accounts double in value, there is no tax associated with a Roth withdrawal. Not only is there no tax on Roth IRA withdrawals, but now there would also be **no tax** owed on their Social Security benefits.

Furthermore, Bill and Karen could still withdraw about $24,000 from their taxable IRA and still pay $0 in tax since they still have their standard deduction to apply against these "taxable" earnings.

Imagine if federal income tax rates double in the future. Or if they just go up by a few percentage points. By converting to a Roth, the Tucker's have protected themselves.

Another tax advantaged/tax free vehicle is permanent life insurance. Money in the policy grows tax deferred and can be accessed tax free via a policy loan or withdrawal. While we don't usually recommend retirees buy life insurance, this feature is a great reason to keep your policy even after you've stopped working. In addition, many new policies today allow you to apply a portion of the death benefit toward long term care costs.

Like a lot of people we meet, the Tuckers rely solely on their accountant for tax advice. But from our experience, many accountants work as tax filers, not tax planners.

Tax planning is one of the most ignored areas of financial planning, and failure to address the IRS lien on savings is ruining people. It is not the job of the IRS to tell you how to lower your taxes. It's your job. If you don't know how, you need to find a professional who does. You won't find him inside a box of Turbo Tax software.

The tax code is very complicated. **Too often people just go along with it**, unaware of the steps that can legally reduce their federal and state income taxes. Failure to address this issue can mean you're not worth anywhere close to what you may think.

Don't Just Take My Word For It:

How to Pay Zero Taxes 2016 by J.K. Lasser

The Power of Zero by David McKnight

Look Before You LIRP by David McKnight

Lesson Number Four: It Will Probably End Badly

"It's paradoxical, that the idea of living a long life appeals to everyone, but the idea of getting old doesn't appeal to anyone."

–Andy Rooney

The first chapter ended with a statement that the future is always likely to be better than the past. For society as a whole, we truly believe that. As for our individual lives, however, we know that life is finite. The Grim Reaper is undefeated. And while modern medicine has made huge strides in fighting heart disease, diabetes, and cancer, we all still die.

The lucky ones will die suddenly, like Tim Russert. Here today living life to the fullest...gone tomorrow. Sad for our loved ones, but much better than dying a slow death where our health declines daily, limited to a wheelchair, incapable of recalling our children's names, and needing assistance to visit the bathroom.

Depressing...isn't it? That's life.

As a society, we are living longer. That is a good thing, but that also means our money must last longer. It means that eventually we will become weak and likely to need help with those things we only want to do for ourselves (custodial care).

Some stats from the National Institute for Health:

- If you reach age 65, there's a 70% chance you'll need custodial care.
- The average nursing home stay is almost three years.
- The average nursing home cost is $70,000 a year.
- Nursing home costs rise at twice the average inflation rate.
- Medicare doesn't pay for Long Term Care.

- Medicaid is available only after you've spent down your assets.
- Most people in nursing homes are on Medicaid, but they didn't start there.

Basically, you have three options when it comes to long term care.

- First, you can self-insure the exposure. Perhaps you have enough money to do just that. Remember...it's $70,000 a year now. At 6% inflation, the price will double in twelve years. If you're married and you get sick, will that leave enough money for your healthy spouse?

- Second, you can rely on Medicaid. Why not? Most do, but, that's available only after you've spent down your own money. If you're married, Medicaid kicks in when you have about $125,000 left. You don't have to sell your house, but the government may attach a lien to it after you die so that it can recoup the cost of your care.

- Third, you can buy long term care insurance. For many people, this is the right choice. Often we hear people say they won't buy it out of fear they'll never use it, and thus waste their money. We're going to let you in on a little secret: the people who go to nursing homes with long term care don't win the game. It's those who have long term care insurance but die peacefully in their sleep, healthy today...dead tomorrow, who win the game.

When your car isn't stolen, do you regret owing auto insurance? Never feel regret for being prudent.

Long term care insurance can be expensive, but a few things can be done to reduce it:

1. Limit coverage to four years. Odds are very high you won't need the policy after four years (you'll die). By limiting coverage to four years, you reduce the cost dramatically over a lifetime benefit policy.

2. Self-insure a part of the cost. If nursing homes in your area cost $200 per day, consider coverage for $150. Be sure to study the long term impact of not being fully insured.

3. Ask your children to pay for it. They are the ones who stand to benefit

from you not spending all of their inheritance on nursing home care.

Whatever you do...have a plan! It's not a matter of if, but when!

Don't Just Take My Word For It:

Long Term Care: Your Financial Planning Guide by Phyllis Shelton

Lesson Number Five: Your Brain is Messed Up

"We have seen the enemy, and he is us."

—Pogo

Perhaps the biggest obstacle (no, not *perhaps*...it really *is* the biggest) preventing financial success is our own brain...our humanness...our emotions.

God gave us many gifts, but if misused, they can be self-destructive.

Consider weight loss. Technically, losing weight is very easy. We simply exercise more and eat less. Yet we are the fattest nation on earth, and weight loss is a multi-billion dollar industry.

Investing is also quite simple: buy when prices are low. Sell when they are high. According to the Dalbar study, we see that simple strategy ignored all the time. People often do the complete opposite.

Let's take Marty McFly's time traveling DeLorean back a few years....to 10,000 BC.

Meet your great, great, great, great, great, great, great, great, great (you get the idea) grandfather. We'll call him Fred. He lives in a cave with his mate Wilma and their children Pebbles and Bam Bam (who they adopted after a T-Rex ate Barney & Betty Rubble).

Life is very simple for Fred and Wilma. Fred wakes up, sharpens his spear and kills whatever he can find. He brings it back to the cave where Wilma cooks it.

Fred is motivated to stop the pains of hunger, cold and predators. He seeks warmth and comfort where he can, but above all else, he tries to avoid pain for his family and himself. He doesn't know it, but Fred has within his brain a survival mechanism that motivates him to behave this way. It is his natural tendency to flee from danger. In fact, all animals have it--another gift from God. Fred doesn't worry about his cholesterol level, his A1C results, or his blood pressure. He merely wants to stay fed, warm and safe. Fred was the original couch potato whenever the opportunity presented itself.

Food, water, safety and warmth...that's all he thinks about. Morality, personal fulfillment, spirituality....these don't matter to him at all. It's a struggle just to meet the basics.

Fast forward to present day. We don't have Fred's worries. Far from it. Food? In the U.S., a major health problem amongst our poor is obesity. Water, warmth...readily available. But the survival mechanism that kept Fred alive until a saber-toothed tiger ate him is still present in our brains. We don't use it often, but it's there...lurking.

Need to lose weight by eating less (painful) and exercising (even more painful)? Forget it. Our brain tells us we're crazy. Stay in bed. Rest. Relax.

Fred didn't care if he lived past age 40, but you do. Rather than helping you though, the survival mechanism is betraying you.

When your stocks fall in value, you experience pain. Your brain tells you that you must do something. You must sell. When what you sold starts increasing in value, you feel worse! You know logically that stocks are likely to rebound, but your brain convinces you that "this time is different."

While the survival mechanism is the worst feature of our psyche when it comes to investing, there are a few others that can be equally destructive:

1. Herding: When we were teenagers, we called it "peer pressure." Our mothers asked, "If Johnny told you to jump off a bridge, would you?" Hey, bridge jumping can be great fun.

When Frank in accounting tells you that everyone is dumping the index fund in the company 401k and loading up heavily on company stock, you need to remind yourself of something. Unless Frank is having secret meetings with the company chairman, he knows nothing more than the rest of the world. All the information about your company is already factored into its stock. Frank is just speculating. Sadly, there were several "Franks" working at Enron.

2. Confirmation Bias: We'd all like to believe that we are objective thinkers, weighing all facts before making a decision or establishing a belief. Sorry...not true. There are things we WANT to believe are true. So much so, we'll ignore any evidence to the contrary. Take an 8 year old girl named Georgie who is committed to believing in Santa Claus. She's heard from classmates that St. Nick isn't real, but every year she finds evidence to the contrary. In her mind, the kids who don't believe are simply the ones who misbehave and receive nothing on December 25th.

For other people, we see confirmation bias in areas like climate change, the Kennedy assassination or the future price of gold.

In 2001, I met a GE engineer who said he had no intention of ever diversifying away from his company stock. "I don't want to hear it," he said to us when we suggested a broader allocation. He was 64, and the stock comprised 100% of his portfolio. In the previous ten years, his net worth had tripled. It seemed invincible.

At that point, the stock was trading at $65 a share. Seven years later, it was worth $8.

When it comes to matters of finance, confirmation bias can be expensive.

3. Gambler's Fallacy: The roulette wheel has come up red the last six times. It must turn up black this time, right? No wait...six times in a row? It has to turn up red a seventh time. It's on a roll.

Of course, both statements are false. The gambler believes that despite randomness, past events influence future events. This is why casinos give free hotel rooms to high rollers. Just don't leave our casino. We know eventually you will give the money back. You believe you have skill, but we know it is pure chance...and the odds of chance favor the house.

We see it with stocks all the time. The market is up, and "experts" call for a "correction." In order for there to be a correction, we must first have a mistake. The "correction assumption" is that stocks are mispriced. Eventually the market will wake up this reality, causing prices to adjust.

It's hogwash. News drives stock prices. Markets will move randomly because news occurs randomly.

4. Anchoring: Back to our GE engineer. His wife saw the potential mistake of holding just one stock, but even she couldn't be swayed toward logic because they knew diversification would trigger taxation. So anchored was she in her belief that taxes are bad, she put herself in a position of eventually owing no tax because they lost most of their portfolio in 2008. Oh, to have Marty's DeLorean.

A successful investor understands that logic doesn't come naturally. He seeks out ways to ensure that when it comes to money, the left side of his brain (where logic resides) stays in control.

Don't Just Take My Word For It:

Predictably Irrational by Dan Ariely

The Behavior Gap by Carl Richards

Lesson Number Six: Rick Perry Was Right

"The real sin with Social Security is that it's a long-term rip-off and a short-term scam."

—Tony Snow

A Ponzi scheme is an investment fraud that involves the payment of purported returns to existing investors from funds contributed by new investors. Ponzi scheme organizers often solicit new investors by promising to invest funds in opportunities claimed to generate high returns with little or no risk. In many Ponzi schemes, the fraudsters focus on attracting new money to make promised payments to earlier-stage investors to create the false appearance that investors are profiting from a legitimate business.

With little or no legitimate earnings, Ponzi schemes require a consistent flow of money from new investors to continue. Ponzi schemes tend to collapse when it becomes difficult to recruit new investors or when a large number of investors ask to cash out.

--United States Securities & Exchange Commission

In the 2012 election primary, pundits attacked Texas Governor Rick Perry for correctly describing the Social Security system as a Ponzi scheme. The system, which began in 1935, then taxed 42 workers for every retiree a maximum total of $30 per year. Today, it taxes three workers for every retiree 6.2% of their earnings (up to $118,550). If you're self-employed, you pay the tax twice.

Money is taken from workers and is transferred to retirees. The rate of return is not guaranteed. Most people will average between two and four percent. Many will lose money if they die before they receive benefits equal to their contributions. Unlike your savings, you cannot leave your Social Security benefits to your children. At least Charles Ponzi gave some investors a high rate of return.

Social Security today is not what it was intended to be when President Roosevelt signed the program into existence. Its original intent was to aid Americans who couldn't take care of themselves, such as widows and orphans. It was never designed to be the sole means for retirement income, which it has become for many Americans today.

In 1935, life expectancy was 62, while the earliest one could collect benefits back then was age 65. On average, you were more likely to die than receive benefits. Ironically, the very first person to receive a check, Ida May Fuller, lived to be 100 years old. These days about 58 million people receive benefits.

Benefit Timing

For many retirees, the question of when to take benefits can be a difficult one. The longer you wait to start collecting, the larger your monthly check. Full retirement age is between 65 and 67 depending on what year you were born.

You can take benefits as early as 62, but receive 25% less per month than if you hold out until your full retirement age. If you wait until age 70 to collect, then you get an extra 8% for every year you wait. In real dollars that means if your full retirement benefit is $2,000 but you elected to take it at 62, you will receive $1,500 each month. Likewise, if you wait until age 70, you will receive $2,700 every month.

Life expectancy plays a major role in determining the timing of your Social Security benefits. The breakeven point for taking benefits at 62 vs. 70 is age 82.

If you had that time machine and knew your expiration date – no problem. Of course, if you delay taking your benefit, it may mean you have to spend more of your savings in the early years of retirement.

Many factors need to be taken into consideration when tapping Social Security.

So what is the future of Social Security? Is it sustainable? What was once a 1% tax is now 6.2%. As fewer people pay in and more are recipients, the percentage could always be increased. The amount of income subject to the tax could be increased, and inflationary increases could be eliminated or decreased. Lots of appealing options...NOT.

No political party wants to broach the elimination of Social Security, and they likely won't. Social Security in its current state isn't at all what Roosevelt had in mind in 1935, so change is always a strong possibility.

Don't Just Take My Word For It:

Get What's Yours: The Secrets to Maxing Out Your Social Security by Laurence J. Kotlikoff, Phillip Moeller and Paul Solman

Lesson Number Seven: You're More Likely to Die Going Down The Mountain

"Everest has always been a magnet for kooks, publicity seekers, hopeless romantics, and others with a shaky hold on reality."

—Jon Krakauer

Let's talk mountain climbing for a minute.

Now I know you're probably scratching your head, thinking: wait, isn't this supposed to be a book about retirement? Well, just bear with me for a moment. Back in 2001, I was inspired by a man named Erik Weihenmayer who became the first blind person to reach the summit of Mount Everest. I was so inspired that I began to research what it would take to conquer this mountain. This is what I found out:

1) It takes a high level of commitment, time and study to prepare to make the trek.

2) The average trip costs $65,000 (and some are over $100,000). Yes, you can do it for less, but in the world of high stakes mountain climbing into "the death zone," do you really want the cheapest guide service?

3) It takes two to three months to get to the summit. If you have the time to train and the money to spend to attempt this feat and you make it to the top of the mountain, you've already accomplished something that most people wouldn't even try. However, even if you make it to the summit, this next statistic was the one that shocked me.

Roughly 80 percent of all accidents that occur when climbing Mt. Everest happen *on the way down.*

This means that despite overcoming unbelievable odds, below freezing temperatures, a lack of oxygen and massive fatigue, **almost all accidents and deaths occur AFTER a climber reaches the summit.**

So what does this have to do with retirement planning? Well, if you think about retirement planning like climbing Mt. Everest, we spend most of our time going up the mountain. This is the "ascent" in mountain climbing and the "accumulation" phase of retirement planning. We build up our assets and investments during our working careers which can span 30 to 40 years. Then, when we reach the summit and it's time to descend down the mountain, a.k.a. the distribution phase of retirement, if you don't have a proper plan or system in place, things tend to go wrong for most retirees, similar to the accidents that occur when Everest climbers make their way down.

It occurred to me that when it comes to retirement planning, we expend so much energy in accumulation that we forget about what happens afterward. Too often, **all our thought processes lie in building up our nest eggs, not in the plans for distributing those**

eggs causing us to have our own accident on the way down the mountain. Oh, if you were wondering... I have never climbed Mt. Everest.

So let's talk about accumulation...

The importance of the accumulation phase to your retirement should be pretty obvious. It is the trek up the mountain. It is during this time that you're building wealth and resources to provide an income for yourself in retirement. Examples of income streams that you can build during the accumulation phase include:

- **Social Security.** A contribution that gets taken from every paycheck you receive. For many retirees, even millionaires, Social Security pay will be a significant income source in retirement.
- **401Ks**. An optional tax-deferred investment that you can make each year if your employer offers such a

program. It's important to make contributions to your 401k each year, as the more you save, the more you'll have for retirement.

- **IRAs.** Each tax season, you have a chance to contribute money to an Individual Retirement Account, or IRA. It may be either pre-tax or after tax depending on the advice of your tax preparer. This money can then grow until the time comes to withdraw it in retirement.
- **Investment Portfolio**. Personal stock portfolios are a popular option for building wealth for retirement. During the accumulation phase, many treat the stock portfolio as a wealth building tool, focusing on higher-risk, higher-reward investments to increase the portfolio's value.
- **Annuities**. Annuities can be another retirement vehicle where you can make lump sum or periodic payments

to an insurance company in exchange for guaranteed income at a later date.

- **Life Insurance Policies**. Some life insurance policies can be effective retirement savings vehicles. For example, you could pay a fixed amount every year (after tax) into a life insurance policy that will grow based on a market index (net of insurance costs, of course) and allows you to withdraw in retirement the principal and any appreciation from the policy effectively tax free. Many think of it as a turbo-charged Roth account since there is no federal limit on how much you can save and it's after tax money going in and tax-free money coming out. Some policies cap your account growth per year (if the market goes up more, you don't get the benefit), but they can also guarantee that you don't lose money if the market index goes down.

As you can see, there are a lot of "tools" to assist you as you ascend up the accumulation mountain. However, as you make it to the summit and start to make the transition to descend down that mountain, there are many pitfalls that can happen along the way and you have to be prepared. Here are three that can have significant effects.

PITFALL #1: RATE OF WITHDRAWAL

In 1994, a financial advisor named William Bengen proposed "the 4% rule." What does the 4% rule tell us? It essentially says that the most you should withdraw from your retirement accounts in any given year is 4%. If you take out more than 4% in any given year, you'll likely run out of money before you die. In other words, you'll have too much life at the end of your money. His theory worked under the premise that the average rate of return on stocks was 8%, while the average ROR for bonds was 6.6%.

Boy, have things changed since then. In fact, there are a number of variables that you need to consider when evaluating exactly how much you should be taking from your accounts in any given year. Life expectancy, rates of return, asset mix, age, and sequence of returns all figure into the equation. Other variables that determine the rate at which you should withdraw your money are: tax rates, Social Security income, pension, and part-time work.

The long and the short of it is this: if you're still using the 4% rule as a guiding principal in your retirement distributions, it may be a bit too aggressive. We may not get the required rates of return in our stock and bond portfolios to justify taking distributions this large.

PITFALL #2: ORDER OF LIQUIDATION

First, let's define order of liquidation. It's the order in which you spend down your various accounts in retirement. If you go about spending your retirement accounts in a willy-nilly or haphazard way, it can dramatically affect how long your retirement dollars last.

There are three basic types of accounts in which you can save for retirement: taxable, tax-deferred and tax-advantaged. How should you go about spending these dollars down? Should you spend all of your taxable assets first? How about tax-deferred? Tax-advantaged? The only way to truly determine the right "order of liquidation" is to sit down with a fiduciary advisor. They have the tools to essentially run every liquidation order that's mathematically conceivable. After performing these calculations, they can tell you the order of liquidation that will maximize your cash flow in retirement. Believe it or not, the impact of taking the wrong order of liquidation can cost retirees millions of dollars.

PITFALL #3: SEQUENCE OF RETURNS

Let's begin again by defining sequence of returns. It's the order in which you experience investment returns in your portfolio. This is very important to pay attention to because if you experience too many negative returns in the early stages of retirement, it could dramatically reduce the lifespan of your retirement assets.

Conversely, if you have positive returns in the earlier years of retirement, and experience those negative returns much later in retirement, then it doesn't have nearly the same impact on your portfolio. If you couple poor returns while taking distributions in those early years, it can do lasting and irreparable damage to your portfolio in retirement. That's why I call it the Everest Effect, because the descent down the mountain can be deadly.

Conquering Everest is not just about making it to the top. It's about making it down the mountain so you can celebrate the accomplishment with friends and family. Retirement is the same. You spend years building up your nest egg and finally make it to retirement but it doesn't stop there. You're going to need that nest egg to last, and it's the decisions you make and things you do while _**in**_ retirement that count.

Don't Just Take My Word For It:

Unshakeable by Tony Robbins
Blind Faith by Edward Winslow

Number Eight: Flat Abs, a low A1C, and Wealth: To get these, you probably need help

"Everyone needs a coach. It doesn't matter whether you're a basketball player, a tennis player, a gymnast or a bridge player."

–Bill Gates

On our own, we rarely perform at our optimal level. A good coach will not only help you achieve excellence, he'll assist in keeping you there. A good coach sees things we can't (or don't want to see). He forces us to leave our comfort zone and to apply logic when emotion is in overdrive. He holds us accountable to ourselves.

One of the biggest failings in the financial services industry is the inability to understand this. The industry is dominated not by coaches (or even advisors) but by commissioned salesmen. They push product as the answer and then go looking for the question. Objectivity is lost, and the client pays the price.

A good wealth coach services his client with a holistic approach and commits himself to putting the needs of the client first.

Over 15 years, we've refined our process to offer such a service.   It's a four step process called the Retirement Rescue.

Step One: Consultation

We begin every first meeting with a simple question: "What will make this a great meeting for you today?"

We want the client to set the agenda. More importantly, we want to know what keeps them up at night.

If on a scale of one to ten (ten means you sleep like Bill Gates, and one means you don't sleep at all), how do you rate your financial situation? If you are a nine or a ten, you're done. Give this book to a friend, and go live your life. No need for any coaching. You are Tiger Woods in 2000.

But if you are more like a seven (or lower), then what has to occur for you to be a ten, aside from winning the lottery? We find that it's rarely about the amount of money one has. The most anxious people we've ever met had significant wealth. Despite that, they were fearful, frustrated and even angry. In some cases, they were victimized by other advisors. To get most people to a ten, it takes a strategy that they have a hand in designing. They require a plan that details fully the pros and cons, and is simple enough that they can explain it to a friend.

Do you need to be a financial expert to be a ten? No. Just like we don't need to know how a hybrid engine works to drive a car. We do need to know how to start the car (which if you haven't bought a car lately, isn't as easy as it used to be). We need to know how to put the car in gear, and how to turn the wheel. We need to know when gas is needed, when to rotate the tires, and when to change the oil. Simple stuff, but it is required.

A well-designed financial strategy answers questions like:

1. How much can I spend during retirement without a strong chance of going broke?

2. What rate of return do I really need on my money, and how can I get it with the least amount of volatility?

3. How can I protect myself from speculation (stock picking, market timing)?

4. How will I deal with catastrophe, such as failing health?

5. How can I legally pay the IRS less?

6. How can I most efficiently transfer my assets at death?

Step Two: Creation

The questions in step one are answered by making you a participant in the plan's design. A good coach listens to what you want to accomplish (I want $X a month for life, after tax, indexed for inflation) and then offers the pros and cons behind the strategy toward achieving that goal. And believe us...there are always cons. Lots of them. You need to know them.

Together we will draw up your plan. How much of your income do you want guaranteed? Before you say "all of it," know that guaranteed usually comes with two costs: low return and less for your heirs.

If you choose to have some or all of your money in a non-guaranteed portfolio, do you fully understand the likely range of returns? What your worst year is likely to be (statistically)? And when it happens (and it will), what will you do?

How much (if any) would you like to leave your children?

How do you wish to handle the cost of custodial care should you need it (and you probably will)?

If you choose to make no changes, what are your chances for success? Are you okay with that?

Step Three: Implementation

Only after the design is fully complete can the plan be implemented. Back when my mom's blood results showed she had too much sugar, she and her doctor together discussed the ups and downs of the strategy: costs, time, denial of certain foods, etc. Once that was outlined, they created a written plan.

Medications can be used to fight illness. The doctor doesn't care where you fill the prescription. He simply wants you to fully take the meds.

In personal finance, products are the medication. And a coach can assist you in acquiring them. Sadly, we too often see financial advisors offer "free" planning. There is no such thing as free. You will pay for it, one way or another. Typically, the "plan" is nothing more than a sales proposal to buy product. "We'll give you a free plan that will recommend you buy a commission-based product from us."

In addition to delivering the written plan, we provide the client with a list of recommendations. With each recommendation, we ask a few simple questions:

1. Do you fully understand this recommendation? Do you know the pros and cons?

2. Are you going to implement it (yes or no...never a "let me think about it")?

3. How are you going to implement it?

No loose ends.

Step Four: Ongoing Coaching and Follow-Up

I have a number of clients from many different walks of life and occupations, and a few of them are pilots. Since we talk about the importance of planning, I asked one of them to bring in a flight plan. He was kind enough to bring one in and that flight plan was over 60 pages long! I asked him why it was so long?

He said because in that flight plan is everything that he needs to know about that plane: Every time it's been written up, everything that hasn't been fixed yet, complaints, history, and every single airport he's going to pass along the way, should he need to make an emergency landing. He knows the weather, the time of the flight, and how long it is.

And here's the thing...it's **all subject to change once he gets in the air.**

You need the same type of thing in retirement. You need a "flight plan" because it's important to understand what you want out of retirement. What are your goals? What do you want to accomplish?

We can help you with the rest...the numbers, the investments, the taxes, the social security, etc.

Retirement is a passage from one lifestyle to another, and it all starts with a plan, implementing the plan, and more importantly REVIEWING the plan at least annually to make sure that you are on track to meet your goals. **Ongoing coaching and follow-up** ensures that you have the peace of mind and confidence that you're going to be okay in retirement. And isn't that the reason you're retiring? To enjoy life?

My Offer to You

If you want to know more about real tax planning, retirement planning, or you just want a second opinion that gives you the peace of mind knowing that your retirement won't be devastated by market volatility, rising tax rates, or other future unknowns, then we can help.

We are offering all readers a Free Consultation. Call us at (502) 339-8255, or visit us online at **www.warren-wealth.com.** We'll show you how we use our **Retirement Rescue Toolkit** to rescue retirement plans for our clients.

You can also attend one of our "New Generation Retirement" workshops by visiting **www.newgenworkshops.com**.

MARCUS WARREN is known among his colleagues, students, and clients as a seasoned and knowledgeable financial professional.

Marcus is passionate about financial education and has a talent to explain financial concepts in an easy to understand manner. Whether it's on the television, radio or in the classroom, Marcus strives to bring the audience to a clear understanding about today's retirement issues with real world financial truths.

As an Enrolled Agent, Marcus is a federally-licensed tax strategist specializing in taxation. Marcus has earned his fellowship through the National Tax Practice Institute (NTPI). He is also a member of the National Society of Financial Educators (NSFE).

His weekly Radio Show, the Race to Retire, can be heard on AM 970 WGTK on Sunday mornings at 9am or by subscribing on iTunes or Google Play.

To learn more about Marcus & his services for helping people overcome financial threats, visit **www.warren-wealth.com**, or email him: **info@warren-wealth.com**.